W9-CFQ-133

American Symbols
AND THEIR Meanings

WASHINGTON
MONUMENT

American Symbols AND THEIR Meanings

Washington Monument

Hal Marcovitz

Mason Crest Publishers
Philadelphia

First printing

1 3 5 7 9 8 6 4 2

Library of Congress Cataloging-in-Publication Data
on file at the Library of Congress

ISBN 1-59084-028-3

Publisher's note: all quotations in this book come
from original sources, and contain the spelling and
grammatical inconsistencies of the original text.

American Symbols
AND THEIR Meanings

CONTENTS

THE IMPORTANCE OF AMERICAN SYMBOLS

Symbols are not merely ornaments to admire—they also tell us stories. If you look at one of them closely, you may want to find out why it was made and what it truly means. If you ask people who live in the society in which the symbol exists, you will learn some things. But by studying the people who created that symbol and the reasons why they made it, you will understand the deepest meanings of that symbol.

The United States owes its identity to great events in history, and the most remarkable American Symbols are rooted in these events. The struggle for independence from Great Britain gave America the Declaration of Independence, the Liberty Bell, the American flag, and other images of freedom. The War of 1812 gave the young country a song dedicated to the flag, "The Star-Spangled Banner," which became our national anthem. Nature gave the country its national animal, the bald eagle. These symbols established the identity of the new nation, and set it apart from the nations of the Old World.

To be emotionally moving, a symbol must strike people with a sense of power and unity. But it often takes a long time for a new symbol to be accepted by all the people, especially if there are older symbols that have gradually lost popularity. For example, the image of Uncle Sam has replaced Brother Jonathan, an earlier representation of the national will, while the Statue of Liberty has replaced Columbia, a woman who represented liberty to Americans in the early 19th century. Since then, Uncle Sam and the Statue of Liberty have endured and have become cherished icons of America.

Of all the symbols, the Statue of Liberty has perhaps the most curious story, for unlike other symbols, Americans did not create her. She was created by the French, who then gave her to America. Hence, she represented not what Americans thought of their country but rather what the French thought of America. It was many years before Americans decided to accept this French goddess of Liberty as a symbol for the United States and its special role among the nations: to spread freedom and enlighten the world.

This series of books is valuable because it presents the story of each of America's great symbols in a freshly written way and will contribute to the students' knowledge and awareness of them. It is to be hoped that this information will awaken an abiding interest in American history, as well as in the meanings of American symbols.

—Barry Moreno,
librarian and historian
Ellis Island/Statue of Liberty National Monument

George Washington was one of the most important American leaders ever. He led the Continental Army to victory against the best fighting force in the world, the British Army, during the War for Independence. Washington was also a great statesman. He helped to create a form of government still used in the United States today, and he served as the first president.

"WITHOUT PARALLEL IN THE WORLD"

*H*e won an important victory at the battle of Trenton when he crossed the icy Delaware River on Christmas night in 1776. He led the troops through the harsh winter of 1777–78 at Valley Forge. He trapped General Cornwallis's Redcoats at Yorktown, ending the American Revolution and delivering freedom and independence to his young country.

He presided over the drafting of the United States Constitution and served as his country's first president. He built the nation's *capital* city. In time, he would come to be known as the father of his country. In the words of Congressman Henry Lee, who served at his side during

9

the Revolutionary War, he was "first in war, first in peace and first in the hearts of his countrymen."

But now, the great father was gone. George Washington died on December 14, 1799, after spending his last few years quietly on his estate in Mount Vernon, Virginia. What could Americans do to honor such an important figure?

Architect Benjamin Latrobe, who had been retained by *Congress* to design many of the government's buildings in the new capital city named the District of Columbia, recommended construction of a *mausoleum* to hold the general's body. He proposed a 100-foot tall *pyramid*, similar to the great pyramids of ancient Egypt that held the bodies of the pharaohs. After some debate, Congress accepted Latrobe's design and made plans to build the pyramid. But due to internal squabbling, Congress never *appropriated* the $200,000 Latrobe said he needed to build it.

Next, Congressman John Marshall of Virginia proposed that Congress construct a vault under the U.S. *Capitol* to house the general's body. Congress appropriated the money and built the vault, but Washington's descendants balked at releasing the body, claiming that George Washington had specified in his will that he be buried at Mount Vernon. The vault beneath the Capitol remains empty to this day. Instead, Washington was buried near his Mount Vernon home.

Members of Congress did take some steps to honor

the president. First, they changed the name of the capital city to Washington, D. C. Next, Congress *commissioned* sculptor Horatio Greenough to fashion a statue of Washington. Greenough created a statue of the general dressed in a Greek *toga* and stripped to the waist, sternly gazing ahead and holding his right arm aloft. The statue shocked Americans. It was displayed for just two years on the Capitol grounds.

By 1833, it was clear that Congress had little idea how to honor the nation's first president. And so, a group that called itself the Washington National Monument Society formed with the intention of building a huge memorial to honor Washington. George Watterston, a former director of the Library of Congress, led the effort to organize the society. He convinced John Marshall, now the

Horatio Greenough's sculpture of George Washington depicted him dressed as a seated emperor wearing a toga. The statue is now part of the Smithsonian Institution's collection.

chief justice of the United States Supreme Court, to serve as the society's first president. The society announced its intentions to erect a monument "whose dimensions and magnificence shall be commensurate with the greatness and gratitude of the nation which gave George Washington birth and whose splendor will be without parallel in the world."

Back in the 1790s, French *engineer* Pierre L'Enfant had worked closely with George Washington to plan the new federal city. The plan included a "National Mall," a 146-acre park intended to contain shrines as well as the president's residence and the U.S. Capitol. In fact, Congress had previously authorized a statue of Washington on horseback erected on the National Mall. But this project fell by the wayside and would not be finished until after the Civil War.

Now, the National Monument Society aimed to use the Mall as the location for the monument.

The society got down to the business of raising money and designing the monument. Society members limited donations to $1 a person a year. They believed that citizens of modest means would not have a chance to contribute to the project if the group accepted large donations from wealthy people. Meanwhile, the society staged a competition for a design. The official rules of the competition instructed the architects to design a monument that would "harmoniously blend durability, simplicity and grandeur."

There was no doubt that the society wanted something tall—a monument that would rise high over the capital, adding a stunning element to the Washington *cityscape*. Watterston called for "the highest *edifice* in the world, and the most stupendous and magnificent monument ever erected to man."

In 1836, the Washington National Monument Society announced that Robert Mills, an architect from South Carolina, had won the competition. Mills's work was well known around Washington. He had been trained by

During the War of 1812, many government buildings in Washington, D.C., were burned by British troops. After the war, Congress named George Watterston its new librarian. Watterston was told to replenish the catalog of books in the congressional library.

Before serving as librarian of Congress, Watterston had been a journalist and novelist in Washington. He was born in 1783 on a ship in the New York harbor.

Under Watterston, Congress obtained the 6,000-volume personal library of former President Thomas Jefferson. He also adopted Jefferson's classification system, designating books by subject matter, for use in the Library of Congress. That classification system remains in use today.

After Watterston lost his job in 1829, he devoted his remaining years to organizing the Washington National Monument Society and raising money for the project. He lived long enough to see the cornerstone laid in 1848, but died in 1854, long before the monument was completed.

Born in Charleston, South Carolina, in 1781, Robert Mills became the first American architect to be trained in the United States. After graduating from the College of Charleston, Mills worked with James Hoban, who designed the White House, and Benjamin Latrobe, who designed many of the government's buildings in the new federal city of Washington, D. C.

Prior to winning the design competition for the Washington Monument, Mills was hired to design a smaller monument to the general in Baltimore, Maryland. The Baltimore monument features a statue of Washington standing atop a tall column.

In Washington, D.C., Mills also designed the treasury, patent office, and post office buildings. Mills designed more than 50 buildings in other American cities.

He died on March 3, 1855, some 30 years before the capstone would be placed atop the Washington Monument, completing the great marble structure he had designed.

Benjamin Latrobe and was eventually named the federal government's official architect.

Mills's design was everything the society had wanted. He proposed a monument with a circular building, called a *pantheon*, 100 feet high and 250 feet in *diameter*. His design included 30 marble columns that would make it resemble an ancient Greek or Roman temple. Above a *portico* serving as the doorway, a 30-foot statue of George Washington would be erected. Under Mills's design, the general would be dressed in a toga, much the way Greenough had envisioned the image of Washington some years before. This time, though, Washington would stand in a chariot drawn by six horses, the lead horse being winged. Inside the pantheon, Mills suggested statues of the signers of the Declaration of Independence as well as other heroes of the American Revolution. In the basement beneath the pantheon, Mills planned a mausoleum that would hold Washington's body.

But that was not all.

Rising from the center of the pantheon would be the structure's most impressive feature—a 500-foot *obelisk* that would be visible for miles, even serving as a navigation aid to ships making their way up the Potomac River. Carved into the sides of the obelisk would be scenes from Washington's military career.

The cost of the entire monument was estimated at $1.25 million—an enormous amount of money in the early years of the 19th century.

There was no question that Mills's design was grand. Watterston was an enthusiastic supporter. He said, "Generations shall call the founders of this glorious work blessed." Others were far less excited by the design. Members of Congress, which would have to give its permission for the society to use the National Mall, decided to suggest their own plan for the monument. Congressman Zadock Pratt headed the effort and recommended a 150-foot domed building that would include a statue of the general and "the busts and statues of the presidents of the United States and other illustrious men of our country, as well as paintings of all the historical subjects which have or may be designed by our artists through the ages to come."

Leaders of the National Monument Society and Congress squabbled over the two sets of plans for the next nine years. Meanwhile, fundraising was lagging. Limiting donations to $1 a person proved to be a failure, so the society lifted the restriction and invited donations from prominent and wealthy Americans who wished to support the project.

In 1845, the society announced it would soon begin construction of the Washington Monument. It would be a scaled-down version of the Mills design that included the obelisk but eliminated the pantheon. The society had collected $87,000 in donations. This was far less than it needed for the project, but members of the organization were confident that once the work started, donations would come flooding in.

And, finally, the society members announced that if Congress would not permit construction on the National Mall, they would find suitable private land somewhere else in Washington. That threat spurred Congress into action. On April 12, 1848, the nation's lawmakers made 30 acres on the Mall available to the society for purposes of housing the Washington Monument.

The 24,500-pound marble cornerstone was laid on July 4, 1848. It was donated by Thomas Symington, a quarry owner from Baltimore, Maryland, and cut into the shape of a block by Matthew G. Emery, a local stonecutter who would one day serve as mayor of Washington, D. C. The stone was shipped to Washington aboard a flatbed railroad car and transferred to a horse-drawn wagon, where it was driven through the city streets on its route to the National Mall. While crossing a canal, a rickety bridge gave way. The stone plummeted down into the canal and became mired in mud.

Word of the accident spread through Washington. When it reached the Navy Yard, about 40 civilian workers were enlisted to hoist the stone out of the mud and cart it to the Mall for the groundbreaking ceremony. Accompanied by a marching band that played patriotic music during the rescue effort, the men from the Navy Yard set up some temporary *hoists* and *winches.* These helped the men lift the huge block out of the canal.

More than 20,000 Americans gathered on the Mall to watch as the cornerstone was placed. Four future presidents were in the crowd that day: Abraham Lincoln and Andrew Johnson, who were then members of Congress: James Buchanan, at the time the secretary of state; and Millard Fillmore, serving then as vice president.

However, the gala atmosphere that welcomed the start of construction quickly gave way to a more somber mood. It became clear that the monument's construction would be plagued by long delays, a lack of funds, fights between members of the National Monument Society and Congress, and just plain bad luck.

UNCLE SAM'S YOUNGEST SON

CITIZEN

KNOW NOTHING.

This is the cover to sheet music for an anti-immigrant song, featuring "Citizen Know-Nothing" as "Uncle Sam's Youngest Son." The political party nicknamed the Know-Nothings (also called the American Party and the Order of the Star-Spangled Banner) derived this name from their practice of secrecy, claiming to "know nothing" when asked about their politics and activities.

THE KNOW-NOTHINGS

The ancient Romans built the Temple of Concord nearly 2,500 years ago. The huge rectangular stone temple, which features tall columns to hold its heavy roof aloft, can be found in Rome today.

In 1854, Pope Pius IX learned of plans in America to erect a great stone monument to President George Washington. Pius had a stone removed from the Temple of Concord. As a tribute to the first American president, he sent it to the United States so it could be used in the construction of the Washington Monument.

It was not warmly received. For months, critics complained that the "Pope's Stone" had no place in an

American monument. After all, the nation's Bill of Rights—which George Washington himself had a hand in writing—specifically prohibited the church from becoming involved in the affairs of the government. And although the Washington Monument was being built with private funds, it was located on the National Mall in Washington—land owned by the federal government.

Nevertheless, the Washington National Monument Society decided to accept the Pope's Stone. That did not end the criticism, however. Many groups—most inspired by a hatred for Roman Catholics—raised more complaints about the stone. One of those groups was known as the Know-Nothings.

In 1849, an organization calling itself the Order of the Star-Spangled Banner started meeting in New York City. Members were sworn to secrecy about the business of the organization. When asked what the group was up to, members always answered, "I know nothing." Soon, they were being called the "Know-Nothings."

By the early 1850s, there was no secret about what the group was up to. It did not want foreign-born people to enter the United States and become citizens. Since many of those *immigrants* arrived from Catholic countries such as Ireland and Italy, the Know-Nothings criticized Catholics.

The campaign slogan of Know-Nothing presidential candidate Millard Fillmore was: "I know nothing but my country, my whole country, and nothing but my country."

When the Pope's Stone arrived at the construction site in Washington, the monument had risen 52 feet from ground level. Officials from the National Monument Society expected trouble from the Know-Nothings, so they ordered the stone stored under armed guard in a *mason*'s shack.

On the night of March 6, 1854, a group of Know-Nothings made their move. They crept up to the mason's shack, surprised the guard, and locked him inside. The Pope's Stone was stolen. It was never recovered. Authorities suspected the Know-Nothings took it to the nearby Potomac River, smashed it into pieces, and hurled the fragments into the water.

Americans were shocked by the theft. The Washington newspaper *National Intelligencer* called the theft a "deed of barbarism." The National Monument Society posted a reward of $100 for anyone supplying information that would lead to the arrest of the thieves. To this day, the crime has never been solved.

In 1982, Pope John Paul II sent another stone to Washington. This time, the stone was inserted into the monument. Etched into the stone are the Latin words *A Roma Americae*. They mean, "From Rome to America."

> In 1927, workers digging a utility trench at 21st and R streets in Washington believed they had unearthed the "Pope's Stone." Authorities have never recognized that stone as the actual Pope's Stone, however.

Though many people liked the idea of a monument to George Washington, progress was slow, and work stopped altogether several times in the 1850s and 1860s. This photo of the the monument was taken in the mid-1850s. Writer Mark Twain once said that the unfinished stump looked like a "factory chimney with the top broken off."

THE MATCHLESS OBELISK

or a brief time the National Monument Society was taken over by Know-Nothings. They fired all construction workers who were Catholics, including the construction superintendent.

Before the Know-Nothings took over the society, it had been hard to raise money to complete the monument, but funds did slowly come in. Unfortunately, for the three years that the Know-Nothings dominated the society, virtually no money was donated, despite a promise by the Know-Nothings to raise money from "those born beneath the Stars and Stripes."

With no money to buy new stones, the construction

superintendent hired by the Know-Nothings used stones that had been previously rejected. Later, when the Know-Nothings were finally driven out of the society, that work had to be torn down and replaced with new stones.

Once the society rid itself of the Know-Nothings, it had to deal with the Civil War. With the Union about to crumble, people didn't seem very interested in donating money to a stone memorial intended to honor the hero of a long-ago war. Also, the government used the National Mall as a campgrounds for Union soldiers. There was little room on the Mall for stonecutters and other construction workers. They soon left to make room for the thousands of tents pitched by the Grand Army of the Potomac.

A tall stone shaft, such as the Washington Monument, is called an obelisk. The word "obelisk" comes from the Greek term "obeliskos," which is a long, pointed tool used for roasting meat.

By the start of the Civil War, the monument had risen a mere 178 feet from the ground. The National Monument Society had just $3,075 in the bank.

After the war, the society began a new fundraising campaign, but again its members were unable to find money to finish the monument. What's more, the Army Corps of Engineers—the unit of the Army that builds bridges, forts, and other structures for the U.S. military— inspected the work that had been done. It found that the

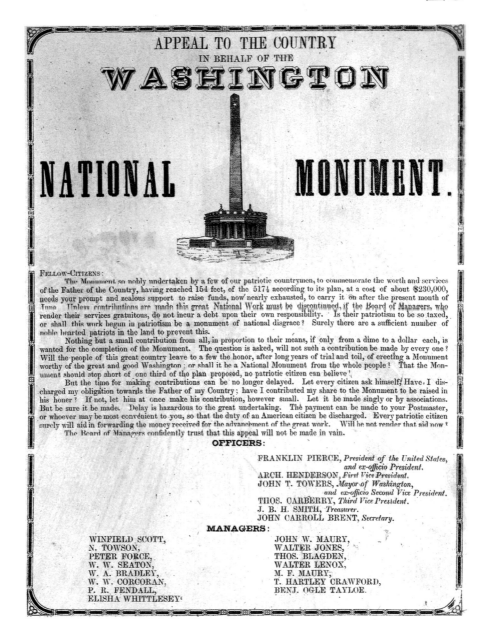

A fundraising letter from the monument society, circa 1853.

foundation would not be strong enough to support the weight of the massive tower. The engineers said that if the monument was completed as planned, and something wasn't done to strengthen the foundation, it would eventually break apart, causing the tall tower to topple over. Work ground to a complete halt while members of the National Monument Society, engineers, and architects argued over what had to be done.

On July 4, 1876—the *centennial* anniversary of the signing of the Declaration of Independence—U.S. Senator John Sherman of Ohio convinced Congress to appropriate $200,000 to finish the Washington Monument. The bill passed unanimously, and President Ulysses S. Grant signed the act into law a month later.

But the money came with strings attached. Sherman insisted that ownership of the monument be turned over to the federal government, and that the work be completed under the direction of the Army Corps of Engineers. Lieutenant Colonel Thomas Lincoln Casey was placed in charge of the project. Casey had spent his entire career in the Army Corps of Engineers. He had headed the efforts to build many of the government's buildings in Washington, including the facilities that housed the State, War, and Navy Departments.

Casey's first problem was to shore up the foundation. The colonel ordered his workers to dig two tunnels below the foundation. They removed hundreds of tons of dirt and filled the tunnels with massive amounts of concrete. The new foundation extended 35 feet out from the monument in each direction, tripling the size of the old foundation.

Next he turned his attention to raising the shaft to its

planned height of 555 feet. He ordered the workers to tear down the inferior stone laid by the crews of the Know-Nothings. That reduced the size of the monument from 178 feet high to about 150 feet. Next, he searched for suitable stone to complete the walls. The marble, he said, "must be white, strong, sound, and must in texture and color so conform to the marble now built in the monument as not to present any marked or striking contrast in color, lustre or shade."

He found construction-worthy marble in a quarry in Maryland, but anyone who visits the monument today can tell Casey was unable to find stone that blended with

Thomas Lincoln Casey was born in a military fort on Lake Ontario, the son of a general. He entered the U.S. Military Academy with every intention of following his father into a career as a battlefield officer. But at West Point, Casey developed a skill for engineering. During the Civil War, Casey was assigned the job of fortifying the coast of Maine in case it became necessary for defenders to ward off attacks from Confederate war ships.

Following the war, Casey was assigned to duty in Washington, where he headed military construction crews charged with erecting many of the military's buildings, including the headquarters for the War and Navy Departments.

After completing the Washington Monument, Casey was promoted to brigadier general and placed in charge of constructing the huge building that would serve as the Library of Congress. He died in 1896 on his way to inspect the construction site.

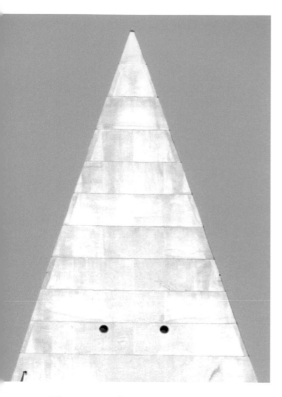

The top of the Washington Monument is more than 550 feet above the ground.

the existing stone already laid in the tower. A change of color is quite apparent at the 150-foot mark.

Under Casey, the work moved quickly. By 1880, the shaft was 176 feet tall. A year later it had grown to 250 feet—nearly halfway to the proposed top.

The budget for the monument also grew. The $200,000 Sherman had been able to squeeze out of Congress soon disappeared. Casey was forced to go back to Congress many times to ask for more money. Ultimately, Congress spent $1,187,710 to finish the Washington Monument.

The monument reached the 500-foot mark on August 9, 1884. The final step was now at hand: construction of the pyramidion, the 55-foot-tall hollow pyramid that would sit atop the structure. On December 6, 1884, Casey personally placed a 9.5-inch by 5.5-inch solid aluminum pyramid on the peak of the *capstone* of the pyramidion. Below, thousands of people gathered on the National Mall to witness the completion of a project that had commenced more than 50 years before, when the

Washington National Monument Committee formed and announced its intentions to finance the construction of a massive memorial to the nation's first president.

When Casey eased the aluminum peak into place, the crowd on the Mall erupted into cheers and applause. On the nearby White House grounds, a battery of soldiers fired a 21-gun salute.

Formal dedication of the monument was held on February 21, 1888—one day before George Washington's 153rd birthday. It was a windy, snowy day in Washington. Nevertheless, a huge crowd turned out on the Mall to watch the ceremonies.

Robert Winthrop, the former Speaker of the House who gave the keynote address when the cornerstone was laid 37 years before, was again asked to give the main speech of the day. Winthrop composed the speech, but was too ill to deliver the address. So Congressman John D. Long read the words Winthrop had written. He said, "Our matchless obelisk stands proudly before us today. The storms of winter must blow and beat upon it. The lightnings of Heaven may scar and blacken it. An earthquake may shake its foundations. But the character which it commemorates and illustrates is secure."

In 1998, the Washington Monument was closed so that an extensive renovation project could begin. More than seven miles of aluminum *scaffolding*, covered with blue netting, were used to surround the monument.

"LOFTY AND ENDURING"

The Washington Monument stands 555 feet 5 $^1/_8$ inches from the tip of the pyramidion to the base on the National Mall. Some 36,000 blocks of marble and granite were used in the monument. It is estimated that the monument weighs more than 81,000 tons.

The pyramidion begins at the 500-foot level. It was fashioned from 300 tons of white marble. Each block of marble in the pyramidion is seven inches thick. The capstone—the block of marble at the very top of the monument—weighs 3,300 pounds. The apex of the capstone is a 100-ounce pyramid of solid aluminum, a rare and exotic metal in the 1880s. The side of the apex

In 1997, Flag Day was celebrated on the grounds of the Washington Monument with the unveiling of a 4,600-square-foot cake baked to resemble a huge American flag. Tourists were given free slices.

that faces east is inscribed with the Latin phrase "Lous Deo," which means "Praise be to God."

Near the base of the monument, the walls are up to 15 feet thick. As the monument rises, the walls become thinner. Just below the pyramidion, the walls are 18 inches thick.

There are 897 iron steps inside the monument, which for years allowed visitors the opportunity to ascend to an observation deck inside the pyramidion. But the stairs were closed in 1976, and now the only way to get to the top is by elevator. Inside the pyramidion, visitors find windows that give them a panoramic view of

At the time the Washington Monument was dedicated in 1885, it was the world's tallest building. The monument did not hold that distinction long. In 1889, the 984-foot Eiffel Tower in Paris (left) was completed. Today, the world's tallest structure is the CN Tower (right) in Toronto, Canada. It rises 1,815 feet into the sky.

Washington as well as the countryside in the nearby states of Virginia and Maryland.

In 1908, baseball player Gabby Street of the old Washington Senators boasted that he could catch a ball tossed out the window of the monument. He missed the first 12 balls, but caught the 13th. It was estimated that the balls traveled 125 miles an hour on their path toward his mitt.

After several people committed suicide by leaping out of the pyramidion, in 1926 bars were added to the windows. Over the years, other people tossed all manner of objects out of the windows—both intentionally and not—often causing injury to people on the Mall below. Finally, the National Park Service installed safety glass in the windows.

In 1949, a circus acrobat walked down the steps, on his hands, in 85 minutes. In 1963, a high school student rode piggyback on a classmate up the stairs in 15 minutes, 30 seconds.

It took 36 years for construction of the monument. The cornerstone was laid on July 4, 1848, and the structure was completed on December 6, 1884. During that time, America fought a Civil War and 11 presidents served in office.

The first American to ascend to the top of the monument on the day of

> **The quickest anyone has walked up and down the steps of the Washington Monument is 19 1/2 minutes.**

Workers on top of the scaffolding around the Washington
Monument during its recent renovation.

dedication on February 21, 1885, was President Chester
A. Arthur. Today, more than 1 million people a year visit
the Washington Monument.

During the 1990s, a structural study performed by the
National Park Service detected several cracks had
formed in the stone, allowing rain water to leak in. When
water enters stone, it has the capability to cause damage
because it will freeze in the winter. When water freezes,
it expands, causing chips to flake off from the stone.

In 1998, a $10 million project to renovate the

Washington Monument began. During the project, workers sealed cracks, removed loose mortar from the 64,000 feet of joints between the stones, and cleaned the 59,000 square feet of interior walls.

Unfortunately, the monument had to be closed during the work. Since January 1998, the monument has been closed four times. Each closure has lasted several months. During that time, however, other improvements have been made to the monument. The windows have been enlarged, offering a better view of the city. A faster new elevator was installed, as well as a better air conditioning system. New exhibits have been added for visitors. Finally, new security measures have been instituted to help prevent a terrorist attack.

During the renovation, workers discovered graffiti painted on an interior wall. It is believed the words were scrawled on the wall sometime during the original construction of the monument.

The graffiti said: "Whoever is the human instrument under God in the conversion of one soul, erects a monument to his own memory more lofty and enduring than this."

The graffiti was signed with the initials "B.F.B."

The National Park Service was never able to identify B.F.B. Instead of erasing those words, the federal government left them where they were found.

Visitors to the Lincoln Memorial in Washington, D.C., look at the Washington Monument. The reflecting pool was designed so that the Washington Monument could be seen from the top steps of the Lincoln Memorial; however, when the Lincoln Memorial was built its foundation had to be extended, so the top of the Washington Monument is not visible in the pool.

STONE UPON STONE

any of the stones that compose the interior walls of the Washington Monument have stories to tell. One hundred and ninety-five stones set along the interior stairway are inscribed with messages, images, and symbols from around the world.

The stones, in their own way, tell the story of the history of America. The stones commemorate such events as Washington's birth and important battles fought during the American Revolution. The feelings of citizens regarding the coming Civil War, the legality of alcoholic beverages, and the rights of Native Americans are also reflected in the stones.

The first inscribed stone arrived in October 1849, sent as a gift from the Alabama State *Legislature*. The message on the Alabama stone reads: "A Union of Equality, as Adjusted by the Constitution." Clearly, the legislators of Alabama intended to send a message that slave-holding states deserved a place in the Union—an issue that would slowly brew over the next dozen years as America moved slowly toward the Civil War.

> Visitors can only briefly view the stones. Since the stairway was closed in 1976, visitors do not have the opportunity to pause along the stairs to read the messages. In the spring of 2001, a new elevator was installed in the monument, featuring windows in the cars that enable visitors to view the stones.

Despite the political message on the Alabama stone, the Washington National Monument Society gratefully accepted it and ordered the stone placed in the monument's interior wall. The Alabama stone can be found about 40 feet above the base of the monument on the west interior wall.

The National Monument Society decided to invite other states to send stones as well. Each stone had to be four feet long, two feet high and 12 to 18 inches thick. Soon, the stones started arriving. Some states sent stones that included just their names and no other message. Some states sent stones that displayed their names as well as their symbols. And some states joined Alabama in sending political messages. The coming Civil War was very much on the minds of Indiana's legislators. That state's stone reads: "Indiana: Knows No North, No South. Nothing but the Union."

> Delaware's stone in the monument was dug out of the battlefield at Brandywine Creek—a battle that George Washington lost.

Some states have more than one stone. In 1849, the stone for Utah Territory was hauled to Washington in a horse-drawn cart driven by members of the religious group known as the Mormons, who had settled the territory. But the stone identified the territory as "Deseret," which was the name the Mormons had given to the region. The stone was inserted into the west wall. When Utah was admitted as a state in 1896, a new stone was sent. Both stones remain in the monument today.

Other states had similar controversies. Montana, for example, sent a blank stone because the state treasury was empty and legislators could not afford to hire an engraver. An image of Montana's mountainous countryside was added later. Mississippi found no source of marble within its borders; legislators had to buy a chunk of marble from Italy to represent their state.

> President Zachary Taylor died of the disease typhus five days after presenting a stone from the City of Washington for an interior wall of the monument.

But states weren't the only entities sending stones. Major cities such as New York, Boston, Philadelphia, and Baltimore sent stones. But so did the little towns of

Honesdale, Pennsylvania; Durham, New Hampshire; and Thomastown, Maine. Fire companies in Cincinnati, New York, and Philadelphia also sent stones.

Masonic organizations—fraternal groups composed originally of the tradesmen who work with stone and mortar—took a particular interest in the monument, since it was their trade that performed the most work on the structure. Over the years, the Masons had evolved from a trade society to an organization of men of social distinction. In fact, George Washington had belonged to a Masonic order. Twenty-two American Masonic organizations sent stones.

Among the foreign nations that contributed stones were China, Canada, Turkey, Wales, Switzerland, and Japan. The Vatican, of course, sent a stone that was stolen. The Greeks sent a stone cut from the Parthenon, an ancient temple that still stands in their country.

In 1919, the states ratified the Eighteenth Amendment to the U.S. Constitution, outlawing the sale of intoxicating liquor. For years leading up to adoption of the amendment, *temperance* organizations—composed of people opposed to the sale of alcohol—made their feelings known by contributing stones to the monument. The stone sent by the Pennsylvania Sons of Temperance reads, "The Surest Safeguard of the Liberty of Our Country is Total Abstinence from All that Intoxicates."

The plight of Native Americans is told by the simple message on one stone. In 1838, more than 18,000

Cherokee Indians were driven off their land by federal troops who forced them to march some 300 miles west to Oklahoma. About 4,000 Cherokees died on the march due to hunger, disease, and exposure to the elements. That march has come to be known as the "Trail of Tears." In 1850, the

The Cherokee make their forced march west from their homeland in Georgia to the Indian Territory, which today is Oklahoma. Thousands of Native Americans died on the "Trail of Tears."

Cherokees sent their own stone to the monument. Its simple message reads: "Cherokee Nation," the name of the society the Cherokees carved out for themselves after they were told they could no longer share their land with white Americans.

Usually, the stones were dedicated during elaborate ceremonies. In the 1920s, President Calvin Coolidge presided over the unveiling of a stone sent by New Mexico, which had just become the 48th state admitted to the Union.

The Washington Monument, Coolidge said, "is built, stone upon stone, forming a solid and harmonious structure, just as America is composed of 48 states joined by the cohesive power of the Constitution."

1799   George Washington dies at Mount Vernon, Virginia, on December 14.

1833   The Washington National Monument Society is formed to finance and build a memorial to the nation's first president.

1836   Robert Mills wins competition to design the Washington Monument.

1848   The cornerstone for the Washington Monument is laid on the National Mall in Washington, D. C., on July 4.

1854   Pope Pius IX makes a gift of an ancient stone to the Washington Monument; it is stolen by the Know-Nothings.

1876   Congress appropriates $200,000 to complete the Washington Monument on July 4; ownership of the monument transfers from the National Monument Society to the U.S. Army Corps of Engineers.

1884   An aluminum capstone is placed atop the monument on December 6, completing construction.

1885   The Washington Monument is dedicated on February 21.

1933   The National Park Service takes over ownership of the monument from the Army Corps of Engineers.

1998   Sheathed in aluminum scaffolding and blue netting, the monument undergoes an extensive renovation.

2001   Renovation of the Washington Monument ends. Improvements include a faster elevator, larger windows, an improved air-conditioning system, and safety measures to guard against terrorist attack. The exterior and interior walls are also cleaned during the $10 million renovation project.

appropriate—to set apart money for something, or to assign to a particular purpose or use.

architect—a designer of buildings.

capital—a city that serves as the official center of a government for a state or nation.

Capitol—the building in Washington where Congress passes laws and conducts other business.

capstone—a stone used at the top of a wall or other structure.

centennial—a 100th anniversary or its celebration.

cityscape—the view of buildings, streets, parks, and other features that make up a city.

commission—a task or matter entrusted to one as an agent for another; to hire someone to do a job.

Congress—the lawmaking branch of the American government.

diameter—the measurement of a straight line passing through the center of a circle.

edifice—a large building with an imposing appearance.

engineer—a person skilled in employing the practical application of a science, such as using chemistry or physics to construct a building.

foundation—the stone and mortar base built below ground that supports a building, bridge, monument, or other structure.

hoists—mechanical devices employing ropes that lift heavy objects.

immigrant—a person who moves from one country to another for the purpose of establishing a permanent residence and becoming a citizen of the new country.

legislature—the governing body of a state, composed of representatives elected by the people.

mason—a construction worker who builds with stones and bricks.

mausoleum—a secure structure intended as a resting place for the dead, also known as a vault.

obelisk—a shaft of stone that tapers at the peak.

pantheon—a public building containing monuments to a nation's heroes.

portico—a roof supported by columns, usually extending out from a building.

pyramid—a structure composed of four triangular sides that meet at a common peak.

scaffolding—a temporary structure erected outside or inside a building to support workers while they conduct repairs.

temperance—a movement calling for the outlawing of alcoholic beverages.

toga—a loose robe worn by citizens of ancient Rome or Greece.

winch—any of various machines or instruments used for hauling or pulling.

FURTHER READING

Allen, Thomas B. *The Washington Monument: It Stands for All.* New York: Discovery Books, 2000.

Chambers, S. Allen. *National Landmarks, America's Treasures: The National Park Foundation's Complete Guide to National Historical Landmarks.* New York: John Wiley and Sons, 1999.

Doherty, Craig A., and Katherine M. Doherty. *Building America: The Washington Monument.* Woodbridge, Conn.: Blackbirch Press, 1995.

Gilmore , Frederic. *The Washington Monument: A Tribute to a Man, a Monument for a Nation.* New York: Child's World, 2000.

Hargrove, Julia. *Historic Moments: Washington Monument.* New York: Teaching and Learning Company, 2001.

INTERNET RESOURCES

Information about the Washington Monument
http://www.nps.gov/wamo
http://sc94.ameslab.gov/TOUR/washmon.html
http://www.dcpages.com/Hwdc/washmo.html
http://www.cr.nps.gov/nr/twhp/wwwlps/lessons/62wash
/62wash.htm

George Washington
http://sc94.ameslab.gov/TOUR/gwash.html
http://memory.loc.gov/ammem/gwhtml/gwhome.html
http://www.whitehouse.gov/history/presidents/gw1.html

The Know-Nothing Party
http://www.newadvent.org/cathen/08677a.htm

PICTURE CREDITS

BARRY MORENO has been librarian and historian at the Ellis Island Immigration Museum and the Statue of Liberty National Monument since 1988. He is the author of *The Statue of Liberty Encyclopedia*, which was published by Simon and Schuster in October 2000. He is a native of Los Angeles, California. After graduation from California State University at Los Angeles, where he earned a degree in history, he joined the National Park Service as a seasonal park ranger at the Statue of Liberty; he eventually became the monument's librarian. In his spare time, Barry enjoys reading, writing, and studying foreign languages and grammar. His biography has been included in *Who's Who Among Hispanic Americans*, *The Directory of National Park Service Historians*, *Who's Who in America*, and *The Directory of American Scholars*.

HAL MARCOVITZ is a journalist for *The Morning Call*, a newspaper based in Allentown, Pennsylvania. He has written more than 20 books for young readers. He lives in Chalfont, Pennsylvania, with his wife, Gail, and their daughters, Ashley and Michelle.